THE TIGUAS

The Tiguas

The Lost Tribe of City Indians

by Stan Steiner

CROWELL-COLLIER PRESS
Division of Macmillan Publishing Co., Inc.
New York
COLLIER MACMILLAN PUBLISHERS
London

Macmillan Publishing Co., Inc.

866 Third Avenue, New York, N.Y. 10022
Collier-Macmillan Canada Ltd.

Library of Congress catalog card number: 77-189728

Printed in the United States of America

10 9 8 7 6 5 4 3 2

All photographs by Stan Steiner unless otherwise noted.

Title page: The aged cacique, Jose Granillo, teaching a Tigua boy how to beat the drum. *Photo: Tigua Tribe (Lee Cain)*

*To those beautiful people,
the Tiguas, who dance on the highway.
And to my beautiful daughter, Suki,
who dances everywhere . . .*

Contents

THE TIGUAS

When the Tiguas have a religious procession,
they cross Highway 80 at this spot.

I

Dancing
on the Highway

In the gentle wind that blows down the highway the lone feather in the headband of the War Captain of the Tigua Indians sways like a radio antenna. He grins. He squints at the diesel trucks that roar past him on Highway 80, on their way into El Paso, Texas. The truck drivers squint at the browned, heavy-set Indian who is standing in the middle of the highway with a rifle in his hands. And beside the War Captain are half a dozen lean and silent young Indians, who at his signal lift their rifles and fire into the sky.

The diesel trucks roar to a halt. Why are the Indians shooting?

On the roadside the old men beat the tribal drums. When the rifle fire has halted the surprised truck drivers and frightened tourists and suburban commuters, the old *Cacique*, the priest, of the tribe of Tiguas leads a procession of one hundred and fifty Indians across the suddenly stilled highway. No one tries to stop them.

It is a strange sight on an ordinary evening in the suburbs of a big city. The waiting motorists gawk.

The Indians are carrying the statue of a saint. Hundreds of years before the highway was built the Tiguas marched in this way, from the mud huts to the mission church, to celebrate the fiesta of their patron, Saint Anthony. On the eve of June 13th they always brought his statue to the church to be blessed. Is it their fault someone has built a superhighway in the path of their holy procession?

In the blue sky supersonic jets from the Biggs Air Force Base zoom by. The young Indians wave.

Some of the Tigua men have worked at the military bases. The younger men of the tribe have been in the Armed Forces. One of them, the son of the tribal governor, was a paratrooper for eight years. He too is marching in the religious procession behind the War Captain on the way to the fiesta.

On the dried hides of their ancient drums the old men beat unending rhythms. The gourd rattles echo on the highway, where the roar of the trucks has been silenced. Solemnly the Tigua Indians of Ysleta del Sur march past "The Cream Cup," a local ice cream parlor and teenagers' hangout. The procession passes the "Happy Hour" bar and the "Blue Goose" dance hall.

A few of the tribal elders begin to chant a song in the old tongue of Tiwa. It is a very sacred march.

The statue of Saint Anthony has been adorned by a beautiful bower of flowers and plants of the desert. He is guarded by the rifles of the warriors of the War Captain. He is carried by the *mayordomos*, the sergeants at arms of the tribe.

Everywhere the statue, or *Santo*, goes the War Captain and his lieutenant fire their rifles in salute and warning to announce his coming.

On the morning of Saint Anthony's Day the Tiguas gathered at the house of the War Captain. Hundreds of Indians and their friends came to the fiesta that lasts all day. But on the holy procession only the most religious come to march.

In the house of the War Captain, in a secret place, are kept the sacred tribal drums, the rattles and old bows and arrows and religious relics that are used in the tribe's ceremonies. The *Wil-a-weka-mede*, or War Captain, is Trinidad Grandillo. He lives just off the superhighway.

The Tiguas are city Indians. In the suburb of El Paso, where they live, they do not have a *kiva*, or church. Nor do they have a *tuh-la*, or meeting house, they say.

And so the people come to the house of the War Captain to be decorated and blessed. The Cacique marks their faces with ocher paint that is the color of a bright mud. He paints the men and boys with a strip across their noses. He paints the women and girls with large dots on their cheeks.

Prayers are said in Tiwa. The people then march to the church, singing.

In the church a solemn mass is said by a Catholic priest. He anoints the people with holy water. When the church service is finished the *mayordomos* fire their rifles in the air, to announce the beginning of "The Chastisement."

On the steps of the church the tribal elders line up. In his hand each man has a whip, or switch, that is made of the green reeds of the willow.

Kneeling on the stone steps, the people tell the elders of the things they have done to hurt one another during the year. The elders pray for them. And everyone promises Saint Anthony that they will harm no one in the year to come. Then the willows lash out! Just to make sure, the elders lightly brush the tribesmen, women and children on both sides of their bodies with the willow reeds. Once this is done they feel the evils of the past have been cleansed by the green leaves. And the dancing can begin.

Joyously the *mayordomos* fire the rifles. The drums talk. One by one the dancers are invited by the Cacique to perform in front of the church while the War Captain lays down his rifle and leads the drumming and chanting.

All morning they dance like deer before the statue of Saint Anthony until everyone is hungry for lunch.

Now the tribal elders walk toward the highway, playing the drums as they go. In a looping and lopping circle the dancers trot along. The loops of the dance are like a human rollercoaster. As each dancer circles the walking band he bows, not to the drummers but to the drum. "He pays his respects to the drum," one of the Tiguas explains.

Once more they cross the highway, with the *mayordomos* firing their rifles. They dance across U.S. Highway 80 in a sort of running trot.

There is a feast at the house of the War Captain. There is Indian bread baked in the outdoor ovens and there are Indian meatballs on which hot chili is poured freely. Cold drinks are served quickly. Everybody eats, the food is free. One week before Saint Anthony's Day the *mayordomos* go from house to house to collect food and money for the feast. The poor feed the poorer. And everyone in the tribe gives whatever he can so everyone in the tribe may eat all he can.

Feasting a little means resting a lot. And even the people who just watch the dancing are tired, so everyone rests. In a little time the drum begins again and the dancers cross the highway once more, led by the *mayordomos* who fire their rifles with renewed energy.

Why do the Tigua Indians stop the cars with their rifles? Why don't they wait for a policeman to direct the traffic, or at least for a red light?

"It is our right. We are in Tigua land. All this place here is Tigua land," says the elected Governor of the tribe, Miguel Pedraza. "My people have lived here for three hundred years. If we fire our guns on our own land, why not?"

That morning there was an argument about the guns. A stranger was driving his car along the roads of the village when the march of the drummers and chanters came by. He almost hit one of the Indians.

"He was driving too fast," the Tigua Governor says. "So the War Captain, he stood in the road with his rifle and he stopped the car. Maybe one of the children would get hurt. The driver got a little bit mad or something. So he started an argument there. After a while I don't know how many policemen came there."

When the procession for Saint Anthony had reached the church the policemen came. The religious dance had already begun.

El Paso's Police Department sent out four patrol cars. They drove into the plaza before the church, ready to stop the fighting. But no one was there but the dancing and chanting Indians. "Maybe there were about 18 policemen there," says the Tigua Governor. "I was busy with the drum and the chanting, and the people were dancing, so really I don't know, but I believe the policemen were trying to stop the dancing. The War Captain talked to the policemen.''

"You can't shoot off shotguns in the city limits of El Paso," the police officer in charge said in a friendly way. "It's against the law. You know that."

"We have always done it," the War Captain said in a friendly way. "We been doing it for hundreds of years."

"Well, you can't do that any more," the police officer said.

"Yes, we can do it," the War Captain said in a friendly way. He smiled. He lifted his rifle and pointed it at the white clouds. "I think I do it," he said. And he shot at the white clouds that floated above the church. "Varrrum!" the rifle roared. Everyone's ears rang with the rifle shot. But the dancers just went on dancing and the drummers did not miss a beat.

In bewilderment the policemen looked at one another. They shook their heads. Around them the hundred and more Indians were quietly chanting and drumming and dancing before the statue of Saint Anthony. The police officer shrugged. He ordered his men back to the patrol cars and they drove out of the plaza in front of the church without another word.

No one cheered. Hardly anyone looked up from their dancing. It was as if nothing had happened.

"We have the right to worship in our own way," the Tigua Governor says. "I don't think they have any right to stop us. Sometimes, mostly every time, we have been pushed around, all the time.

"Anyway, we keep on dancing until we finish it, the dance." The Governor smiles.

II

The Secret Masks

So powerful were the masks of the buffalo dancers, with their hairy faces and great horns, that the old men say if a stranger looked at them he might become blind. Or he might die. In the old days it was the task of the War Captain to hide them. He had to hide them from the eyes of strangers.

The masks of the buffalo, the *aweloo*, are hidden. No one has ever seen them but the Tiguas.

Where are the *aweloo*? The buffalo masks have

vanished just like the buffalo. Long ago they were all lost. No one knows where they are, the old men say.

Once an anthropologist asked a War Captain what had happened to the masks. The *aweloo* had been destroyed in a house that had burned to the ground, replied the War Captain. He said this with a straight face. He would say no more.

So the anthropologist asked the old men if they knew. He was told that only the dead remembered the *aweloo*.

And then, one day, he met two *aweloo* dancers, who were very much alive. They told him about the dances. They told him about the buffalo masks. He did not know whether they were telling the truth. No one who knows the secret of the *aweloo* will tell it. If they did the gods would be angry, for if a secret is told it is lost.

Is the Dance of the *Aweloo* performed in the secret of the night, in secret places, in the city of El Paso?

No one knows. No one will ever know but the Tiguas, and they will never tell. If the knowledge of their sacred songs and dances becomes known to strangers, the knowledge may be taken away, they say. And nothing will be left for the young Tiguas that belongs just to the Tiguas and no one else.

You have taken everything else, they say. Now you want to take our religion away.

When the young warriors come home from the modern wars some of the tribes now sing the old war songs. They dance the old war dances. In some tribes the scalping songs are sung once more to bless the veterans of the United States Marine Corps.

Eyes of strangers do not often see these things. The singers and dancers of the old warrior ways try to hide their religious rites from strange ears and eyes.

The old ways have not died. Sometimes it seems that these ways of long ago have been forgotten. But they have merely changed, say the Tiguas.

In the suburbs where they live the Tiguas still have a tribal society. The Cacique is still the spiritual leader of the tribe. He is still known by the old Tiwa name of *Ai-ka-mede.* The War Captain still leads the tribe in battle, although it is now a battle against the attacks of highway traffic. He too has his old name of *Wil-a-weka-mede.* And the Tigua Governor still has the ancient cane given him by the King of Spain. It is the symbol of his reign. He too has his old name of *Tu-wata-a-bode.*

Strangers do not know these things about the Tiguas. They have kept their old beliefs to themselves. They turn off their television sets and sing the chants and dance the religious dances and weave beaded belts, not for the tourists but for themselves. They do these things in secret.

And they pray to their gods that are as old as their land. They have kept their faith.

When they come home from their work in the modern plants and office buildings of the city they become Pueblo Indians once more. They have a secret self.

Once in a while the Tiguas do appear in public. Sometimes they even wear tribal dress. The old Cacique appeared in 1916, when he blessed the Elephant Butte Dam on the Rio Grande, one of the first irrigation projects in the Southwest. He dressed in his buckskins for that occasion. Then he and the tribe once more retired into secrecy.

It was twenty-two years later, in 1938, when the Tiguas again appeared on the national scene. The President of the United States, Franklin Delano Roosevelt, was then visiting the Texas Centennial Cavalcade. And the Cacique went to greet the President. He declared Roosevelt an ''Honorary Cacique'' of the tribe.

Then once more the Tiguas retreated into the silence of their homes. And they performed their ceremonies quietly, and alone.

In the old days, some say, they would smoke a pipe of bone or clay before a ceremony. The ''peace pipe'' the white men called it, because the Indians said they ''made peace'' with the world, by smoking the pipe. One of the tribal leaders would blow smoke in the four directions of the wind and the world as a sign of peace with the four corners of the earth. They would then be in harmony with the earth and God, they said. And then the ceremony could begin.

Nowadays the pipe of bone is no longer smoked before a ceremony, they say. Instead they smoke cigarettes.

When the old Cacique, Tomas Granillo, was alive, he would begin the tribal meetings by passing a cigarette around the room. It was like smoking a "peace pipe." Everyone puffed on the cigarette until they were in harmony.

And the older men still remember when they went hunting, they always smoked a cigarette in this way before the hunt began. They blew the cigarette smoke in the four directions of the wind and the world, for "luck," they say. Just the "peace pipe" had changed, not the ceremony.

Of course they do not do that any more, they say. And they wink!

Living in a city full of strangers for so long the Tiguas have learned to disguise their ceremonies. And to hide their secrets. But the Tiguas are still Tiguas because they have not let the strangers take their secrets away from them.

Some of the secrets of the Tiguas are so secret they do not know them themselves. And if they did, they would not tell.

III

The Lost Tribe

In the summer evenings the Governor of the Tiguas sits at his dining-room table and strings a beaded belt. He sometimes watches television, but not when his son, a veteran of the paratroopers, has come over to work on his beaded buckskin jacket. On his home-made loom the father weaves the beaded belt into old and beautiful designs. When it is finished he will wear the rainbow of beads at the tribal dances. His hands work deftly and quickly, for his old fingers have grown strong from driving a bus for more than a quarter of a century.

The tribal leader is a school-bus driver, for the Ysleta High School.

One year, not long ago, the boys and girls on his school bus got together and gave the Tigua Governor a plaque. It read:

PRESENTED TO MR. MIKE PEDRAZA,

OUR FAVORITE BUS DRIVER, FOR HIS PATIENCE,

TOLERANCE AND UNDERSTANDING OF US KIDS.

THANKS MIKE.

THE KIDS

The school newspaper hailed him as the "helper of the tribe of Tigua Indians." The students did not seem to know that their "favorite bus driver" was not just the "helper of the tribe." He was the Governor.

Many of the boys and girls did not even know he was an Indian. They did not recognize a modern Indian.

After all, he does not dress like those Hollywood actors who pretend to be Indians on televison. He does not have to act like an Indian because he is one. He does not wear his beaded belt on the school bus. He looks like a bus driver.

"Some of us Indians are truck drivers. Some are farmers. Some work in the fields, chopping cotton. Some work for the schools," says the Tigua Governor. "We work to make our living, like everyone.

"I have a brother who builds houses, like a contractor. I have a brother who works for the water company. I have a brother who works for the gas company. He works in town, in that big, tall building. He works there all the time, about twenty years. He is my brother too."

City Indians? Who ever heard of a tribe of Indians living in the suburbs of a city and working downtown?

It may seem strange, but it isn't. Nowadays half of the Indians in the United States live in the cities and suburbs. The Tiguas are not the only tribe of city Indians, although they were one of the first.

There may be twenty thousand Indians living in New York City. Chicago has twenty-five thousand. Denver has at least as many. San Francisco may have more. In Seattle, some say, there are thirty thousand. Los Angeles may have forty thousand. No one knows how many Indians are living in Washington, D.C., or Oklahoma City, or Miami Beach, or Hollywood.

Even the Indians who live in cities do not know how many there are. Many of them cannot recognize themselves.

An Indian in the city sometimes becomes invisible. He wears the costume of the city tribes of white men. Like everyone else, he learns to perform the tribal rituals of coffee breaks and the war dances of the commuters on the freeways.

But, "We are still Indians," says Miguel Pedraza. "Always!

"Just because we live in the city doesn't mean we

aren't Indians," says the Tigua Governor. "Just because we talk English, or the Spanish, and talk not much of our own language, Tiwa, doesn't mean we don't have Indian blood in our veins.

"We have Indian hearts. We will always be Tiguas," he says.

The neighbors of the Tiguas do not always see it that way. Many of them do not see the Tiguas at all. Some of the people have next-door neighbors who have lived beside a Tigua family all their lives but who do not know that the family that lives across the backyard from them are Indians.

Former Senator Ralph Yarborough of Texas has described how invisible the Tiguas have been to some: "I went to El Paso, Texas, in 1927, as a young lawyer. As I reached there, the Tiguas were having their fall harvest dance. I learned at that time, as most Texans do not know, that there was a tribe of Tiguas there and that they have been there since 1682."

Yet many people thought that the Tiguas had died long ago. Like the herds of buffalo, the tribe was supposed to have vanished.

A Lieutenant Whiting of the United States Army visited the Tiguas in 1847. He mournfully wrote to his commanding officer, General Totten, that the tribe was "fast dwindling away, and but a few years will pass before the last altar fire of their race will be extinguished."

The eloquent Sam Houston, who was the first president of the Republic of Texas, in 1836, was even gloomier. He wrote of the Indians: "As a race they have withered from the land. Their arrows are broken and their springs are dried up; their council fires have long since gone out. . . . Ages hence, the inquisitive white man, as he stands by some growing city, will ponder on the structure of their disturbed remains, and wonder to what manner of person they belonged. They will live only in the songs and chronicles of their exterminators."

He was wrong. One hundred and thirty years later the Tiguas were still living in the "growing city."

Yet the people believed Sam Houston. They thought the Tiguas were gone.

The historians believed it too. In *The Indians of Texas*, a huge book published by the University of Texas in 1961, there are hundreds of pages about the tribes of the state, but just one sentence about the modern Tiguas. It says they are as good as dead, "and are presumably extinct in a cultural sense."

One university professor sadly wrote the same dirge to the lawyer of the Tiguas in 1965: "I have been told by several anthropologists in New Mexico—and by others—that the El Paso group (of Tiguas) was extinct."

In Washington, D.C., the United States Government refused to recognize the Tiguas' existence. How could it, since the tribe was "extinct"? So everyone agreed that the Tiguas did not exist. They were dead. They had vanished. They were the Lost Tribe.

Everyone agreed but the Tiguas. They thought they were still alive.

It was true they had fooled everyone. They had disguised themselves. They wore the white man's costumes over their Indian hearts. As city Indians they had become invisible.

Living in the city was nothing new to the Tiguas. They had been living in cities for almost one thousand years. They had come from one of the oldest cities in America, the legendary city of Gran Quivira in the Mountains of the Apple.

IV

The Ghostly Ruins of Gran Quivira

The stones sleep. In the mornings the mist rises in the mountains like a thousand ghosts. And the mountains themselves loom over the desert like shadows. Hidden in the Mountains of the Apple, the Manzano Mountains of New Mexico, the ruins of the city stand as they did on that day the city was abandoned three hundred years ago, when the men, women and children suddenly fled in terror.

Now it is still. There is nothing living in the ruins. A

sign of the Park Service warns, DON'T STEP ON THE RATTLESNAKES!

"In the old days the old Cacique always ended the prayer for our fiesta with the words, 'And remember this: Our people came from Gran Quivira,' " says the Tigua Governor.

Where is this lost city? Has he ever been there?

No, says the Governor, he has never seen the ruins. But he knows it is his people's ancestral home that was destroyed centuries ago. There is dust there now where the great buildings stood. No one goes there now but the tourists. No one lives in Gran Quivira any more but rattlesnakes, he says.

Then how does he know the Tiguas came from there? Where is it written?

He knows, the Governor says. In his closet he has a map which he takes out and lays on his dining-room table. "It is here," he says, and his finger points to an unmarked spot on the map which is exactly where the ruins of Gran Quivira rise in the distant mountains. The Governor may never have been there, but he knows the place. He remembers it by heart, from the old legends in his tribal memory.

"In our hearts we do not forget our past," he says.

When most of Europe was inhabited by wild and primitive tribes the forefathers of the Tiguas were living in towering apartment houses in the Mountains of the Apple. They had built great cities when London was still a village and New York was mostly a swamp.

Hundreds of years before the explorers from Europe set sail for the unknown New World, the ancient Indians had explored half the continent and had settled beyond the deserts in the beautiful valley that they now call Gran Quivira.

The houses of the first settlers of Gran Quivira were built in A.D. 800!

Year by year the houses grew, until by 1100 they had become a village. By 1300 the village had become a pueblo, or small city, where many families of Tiguas lived together in large stone apartment houses.

In 1540, when the knights of old Spain began to march back and forth across the deserts of the Southwest, conquering everything in sight, they were surprised by the size of these ancient, but modern, towns. There were then at least eighty of these pueblos. Some say there were many more that are now buried in the desert sands.

An early Spanish explorer wrote home in wonder of these cities "composed of many-storied houses," as high as "four storys," and decorated with jewels. He was awed by one city that was "larger than the city of Mexico" of the Aztecs.

The Pueblo Bonito, the Pretty Town, was one of the largest. It amazed the conceited Europeans. All in one building, this single apartment house had more than eight hundred rooms and thirty-two *kivas*, or churches. Unbelievably, the building of the Pueblo Bonito had been finished in the year 1102.

One of the old pueblos the Europeans "discovered" was seven stories tall. The most spectacular, however, was the Hopi pueblo of Oraibi. It had been built by master architects in the year 900, on the very edge of a flat mountain known as a mesa, the Spanish word for table. The windows of its houses are higher than those of any skyscraper apartment house in New York or Chicago or Los Angeles. And people still live in Oraibi to this day.

But, of the ancient cities, one of the most mysterious was Gran Quivira.

Its beauty was famous. Gran Quivira was a fabled city, the Xanadu of the desert. The housing projects of the city covered seventeen acres. And these housing projects were built of stones that shimmered in the mountain air like jewels, rising in tiers on the hillsides in layers of history.

There were twenty housing projects in the city. There were terraces and garden apartments that opened onto sunny plazas. There were numerous churches and workshops and warehouses and lumber yards and communal kitchens that everyone shared freely. There were hundreds and hundreds of rooms. No one knows how many. The dust of centuries has buried most of them.

Some think one thousand people lived there. Some think more, some think less. No one knows.

These houses of stone were built by expert masons, who had no cement. No nails. Few tools. Yet so strong and well built were the houses that most are still standing after nearly one thousand years of mountain storms and desert winds.

A man who stood on the doorstep of his apartment in the pueblo of Gran Quivira gazed down at farms that stretched for miles into the valley below. The farms turned the desert green. Crops of beans and corn and squash were plentiful.

There were no lakes, nor any water in the valley. But the farmers watered their fields ingeniously. They dammed the arroyos (canyons) and dry washes. They dug irrigation ditches in the dry sand. Not far from the village they dug shallow wells where the women filled their jugs with mountain water that sparkled like champagne.

It was possible, the people of Quivira proved, to get water even from the stones of the desert.

Quivira! the word was magical to the conquistadors of Spain. Wherever the conquerors roamed the people told them stories of the great city of Quivira. And of the wealth of the people who lived there.

Here was the Eldorado, the Paradise, they sought, the conquistadors thought. They had been searching everywhere for the fabled city of gold.

And so in 1541 the Knight of Eldorado, the bold and romantic Francisco Vásquez de Coronado, marched his army all the way to Kansas, looking in vain for the gold of Quivira. He did not find it. The Conquistador never would have believed that the wealth of Quivira the people told him about consisted not of gold but of happiness.

Laughter greeted the conquerors. The people of the pueblos thought the weary knights in their sweaty armor who marched back and forth through the sweltering deserts were fools.

In one modern pueblo they still tell the story of how, when the conquistadors came in 1540, the tribal elders sent out the village idiot to give them directions.

The conquistadors had expected to find savages and gold. Instead they found an ancient civilization, as old if not older than their own, and cities of skillful builders and sophisticated artists. A Spanish priest wrote in 1539 that these cities were "thickly settled with intelligent people." He was quite dumbfounded.

So they named the people Pueblo Indians. That meant Town Indians, or City Indians. *Pueblo* is simply the Spanish word for a "town" or "city."

And they named the city of Gran Quivira the *Pueblo de las Humanas*—the City of Human Beings. It was the conquistadors' way of saying that this was one of the friendliest and most peaceful of the pueblos. They had little need to be warlike. They had everything they needed in their beautiful city.

But then tragedy struck. In the summer of 1666 a drought dried up the valley.

The water holes and shallow wells of the pueblo evaporated. Within a few years disease and drought were ravaging Gran Quivira. One year, in 1668, more than four hundred men, women and children are said to have died of hunger and illness.

Many people had come from neighboring pueblos to escape the conquistadors. In Gran Quivira they had found refuge. There was now not enough food for them.

Worst of all were the desperate raids of the Apaches. These hunters of the plains had acquired fast horses from the conquistadors. On the plains the drought had struck too, and the invading Spaniards had driven the Apaches from their favorite hunting grounds. In hunger and frustration the Apaches raided the farms of the Pueblos, for they too were starving.

The exodus began. In the year of sorrow, 1675, the beautiful and great city of Quivira was abandoned forever. And it was doomed to become a ghostly ruin.

And so the ancestors of the Tiguas sadly left their city, but they never forgot it. They sang about it in a melancholy song.

> *My home over there,*
> *Now I remember it.*
> *And when I see*
> > *the mountain far away*
> *Oh, then I weep.*
> *Oh, what can I do?*

The people went down the mountain into the desert, on to the Journey of Death.

V

The Journey
of Death

They walked through the desert on foot. It was a fifty-mile walk to the great river, the Rio Grande, where they hoped to find peace.

They walked into a war!

On the river banks were the pueblos of the Peaceful People. It was an idyllic land. "The river flows through a wide valley seeded with fields of corn and dotted with groves of cottonwood trees," wrote a soldier of Coronado, Don Hernando de Alvarado. And the people were "good people, more devoted to agriculture, than to war," he happily added. That was before the war began.

It was a valley of dreams. Of the peaceful people the noble Alvarado wrote: "They grow crops of corn, beans, melons and turkeys in great abundance. They wear clothes woven of cotton, leather made of the hides of cattle, and coats made of turkey feathers, and they wear their hair short." (Knights, in those days, had long hair, often down to their shoulders.)

The hungry and ragged refugees from the pueblo of Gran Quivira came into this valley seeking peace. Refuge was offered to them, and food.

But they found no peace. Instead they found death.

In the beginning the peaceful people had welcomed the warlike knights of Spain, as they did everyone, with feasts of friendship. And with music. That was their way.

When the "White Men with Whiskers" rode into the valley on their armored horses, the old men of the pueblos had come bearing gifts. They gave them "even the cotton garments they wore," said one soldier of Spain. They gave the strangers food to eat and land to camp on. They danced to the music of their flutes and drums in welcome.

"The Indians came from the neighboring provinces to offer me peace," wrote Alvarado in delight.

And if the Franciscan fathers who came with the conquistadors wished to erect huge crosses, the people were respectful. They adorned the crosses with "roses and plumes." Even the strange god of the strangers might be holy. There was an old prophecy that foretold that one day the gods would send "White Men with Whiskers" to the pueblos. Maybe these strangers had been sent by the gods.

So the warriors held their bowstrings. They feasted with the strangers, in peace.

But the conquistadors had not journeyed across the seas seeking friends. They sought gold. When they found none, they demanded that the men of the pueblos work in their mines as slaves. From their armored horses they looked down on the peaceful people in contempt. They thought that these gentle men must be too timid and weak to resist. So they enslaved them.

And then there was bloodshed.

In one of the pueblos on the Rio Grande that the conquistadors had named the Tiguex, or Tiguas, the haughty conquerors demanded more food and cloth than the people had. They then demanded that the women of the pueblo be given to them as servants.

No! the chiefs replied. We will not give you our women!

On their armored horses the knights of Spain rode into the quiet pueblo and took two hundred men prisoner. Into the stockade they threw them. Surrender the women, they demanded, or we will burn the men at the stake. We will burn them alive!

When the men heard this they broke out of the stockade. They ran for their lives. They could not escape the horsemen and many of them were slaughtered.

The word was then given: No longer trust the "White Men with Whiskers." They have not been sent by the gods.

At the quiet pueblo of Acoma, the serene City in the Sky, the warriors fought when the conquistadors approached. They fought hard, but they lost. The noble Don Juan de Oñate, who commanded the Spaniards, did not kill the warriors in revenge. He was a cultured man. He merely ordered that the right leg of every man of Acoma who was over the age of twenty-five years be cut off below the knee.

Elsewhere the conquistadors were not as cultured and lenient as the noble Oñate.

It had to happen; the peaceful people revolted. Whenever man enslaves his fellow man, sooner or later there is a revolution of the slaves.

The Pueblo Revolt of 1680 began just five years after the refugees from Gran Quivira came into the river valley seeking peace.

One by one the pueblos got together. They held a council of war that was known as the All Pueblo Council. Up and down the river valley the warriors took up their bows and lances. They attacked the surprised conquistadors and defeated them. They burned down the churches and tore down the crosses they had helped erect. They freed their slaves and proclaimed they would drive the strangers from their land.

Governor Don Antonio de Otermin and his Spanish army were trapped in Santa Fe by the triumphant warriors. Yet they were allowed to escape. The people of the pueblos did not wish to slaughter them. All they wanted was their freedom. So they let their tormentors flee to Mexico.

In the pueblo of Isleta the bedraggled knights of Spain paused to refresh their families and horses. The people of the pueblo, some of them Tiguas, were, however, "going over to the enemy" and "making many other dangerous demonstrations," wrote the soldier Dominquez de Mendoza, who commanded the encampment. Once more the fearful conquistadors hurriedly fled, southward toward El Paso, two hundred and fifty miles away.

On the journey through the deserts they took with them 315 "Christian Indians" to carry their supplies and armor. Among these were some of the Tiguas from Gran Quivira who were living at Isleta.

Some say the Tiguas were forced to go with the Spaniards, as prisoners. Some say the Tiguas went willingly, as traitors.

The old men, wiser in the ways of the Tiguas, say neither is true. For the once proud and prosperous people of Gran Quivira were merely seeking a land of their own, they say. They were not happy at Isleta.

They had come five years before, as strangers. They were treated as beggars.

Now they saw a chance to leave with the wagon trains of the defeated conquistadors. They went along, in the hope that on the way they might find a home of their own.

The deserts that stretched before them were an inferno of sand fifty miles wide. There were no towns. There were no roads. There were no water holes. Along the wayside were the skeletons of men and animals that had died trying to cross the parched earth. Their bones were bleached white by the white, hot sun.

The *Jornada de Muerte*—the Journey of Death— the conquistadors called the desert.

And the Tiguas walked through the Journey of Death on foot. It was as deadly then as it is today. Hundreds of years later, during World War II, the first atomic bomb was exploded not far from where the Tiguas walked. The Journey of Death is now a missile range.

When the foot-weary Tiguas reached the grassy fields on the Rio Grande, at El Paso, they fell in exhaustion. Or thanksgiving. It was here, they decided, that they would settle.

But their wandering had not yet ceased. Nor were they yet at peace.

The exiled Governor Otermin was determined to reconquer his lost kingdom of New Mexico. In the winter of 1681 he set forth with an army that included thirty Indian conscripts from the Tigua tribe. Once more they walked through the Journey of Death. On arriving at the pueblo of Isleta, the would-be reconquerors, or reconquistadors, found that the rebellious Indians had "converted the church into a cattle corral," and then had fled.

It enraged the Royal Governor. He angrily ordered his soldiers to burn the entire pueblo to the ground.

The burning of Isleta took all day. It is hard work to destroy a village. Not one house, not one shrine, was not blackened by the flames. By late afternoon the fires had turned the sky black.

All those of the pueblo who survived the fire, some 385 people, were taken prisoner. They were brought to El Paso as trophies of war.

Once more the Tiguas were forced to walk through the Journey of Death. The Spaniards rode on their horses. But the Tiguas went on foot. Some of the men of the tribe had now walked through the desert three times. Some had walked more than one thousand miles.

They had been driven from their great city of Gran Quivira. They had been driven from their refuge in the pueblo of Isleta. Where could they go now? They were birds of the desert.

And so when they came to the grassy fields of El Paso, on the banks of the Rio Grande, on the fifteenth of February, 1682, they settled there. They decided to hide inside the buildings of the town. They disappeared, in the disguise of city Indians. For almost three hundred years no one, not even their next-door neighbors, knew that the Tiguas were living there.

VI

Mystery of the Hueco Caves

In the dry and fiery desert to the north of the town there is a mysterious and cool lake.

On all sides of the lake there is a circle of mountains. The sun is hot. The land is parched. No one on the road that goes nearby would dream that there is water in the midst of this desert. It is in a hidden valley of cool and deep caves, and secret waterholes, and winds that seem to blow out of nowhere, and ancient cave writings. The Tiguas say it is a sacred place. And they call it the *Hueco.*

The stagecoaches to the West came this way. Riders
on the overland stage to California rested here, while
the drivers changed and watered their horses by the
lake. In the valley there are ruins of an inn and old
corrals.

On the rocks of a cave behind the abandoned corrals
there are strange drawings. A row of arrows is painted
on the rocks. It leads to a water hole deep inside the
cave.

And the names of soldiers are carved in the rocks.
The rocks were postcards for the troops of the U.S.
Cavalry. In the pioneer days soldiers had to ride with
the mails. One gun-slinging postman of that day
carved a huge Seal of the United States, five feet wide,
on these rocks. The mail delivery must have been late
that day.

Of all these rock carvings, the most mysterious is
that of a white whale. It is a great monster, two feet
long. And why is this fish lost in the desert, hundreds
of miles from the sea? The white whale is doomed to
swim eternally upon its sea of stone, going nowhere.

The farther you go into the cave, the more Mexican
names are carved on the rocks, and the fewer Yan-
kees. But deeper yet are the signs of ancient Indians.

It is a journey into history. The cave is a history
book. On the roof of the cave are the drawings of
hunters and warriors and gods of the people who lived
here hundreds of years ago. Some of these pictures, or
pictographs, are hard to "read." But the Tiguas can
"read" them. They read them as if they were reading

Above: The Tiguas dance and chant, and the tribal religious leaders perform their ancient rituals on these church steps; in the niche is a statue of St. Anthony, the Tiguas' patron. *Below:* Ysleta High School boasts it is the "Home of the Indians," but that means the football team. Tigua teenagers go there, but the tribe wants its own school.

Left: Ruins of the fabled city of Gran Quivira, where the Tiguas built great apartment houses hundreds of years ago, and of the church the Spanish built there. *Below:* The church at Isleta Pueblo in New Mexico was built in 1613. The Tiguas prayed here when they came to Isleta in 1675.

Above: The mysterious lake in the middle of the desert—the Hueco Tanks—that the Tiguas say is sacred land to them. *Below:* The white whale carved at the entrance to one of the Hueco Caves.

stories of the past. They even know where the row of arrows point.

"My people paint the arrows on the rock long time ago," says Miguel Pedraza, the Tigua Governor, "so, always they can find water to drink.

"Here there is water, I think," he says. "Let's see!"

An overhang of rock hides the pool in the cave from the eyes of strangers, but the old man knows the pool from memory. He follows the row of arrows with his finger until his finger points to an unseen spot. He is right. The pool is there.

The pool is full of beer cans and soda bottles. Campers and tourists have thrown their garbage into the once clean water.

"Last time I come here, I drink some of the water. It was fresh." The Tigua Governor sighs. "No more!

"I come here many times. There is a cave I call Pedraza's Cave a little ways down. My father's name is written on the cave there. So I call it Pedraza's. I don't know for sure who lived there long before, but I know my father lived there some time back. Not only him. As far as I know there were about eight Indians living together with him. He wrote his name on the rock," he says.

"I come here when I was a little boy," the old man says. "My people been coming here a long time. Then it was clean everywhere. No more!"

On the rocks above the cave there are footholds carved in the mountains. The steps of these rock-ladders go straight up the steep face of the mountainside. With a sure-footed step the Tigua Governor walks up the incline. He climbs swiftly. The old man climbs like a young man.

The footholds are good ladders. But they were not carved by men. The winds of the desert carved them.

It is windy on the mountain top though there is no wind in the valley. The wind is strong, so strong that a man has to brace his two feet firmly. Even then the force of the wind bends his limbs. The cliff drops for two hundred feet in a sheer incline on the other side of the mountain.

One wrong step would mean quick death on the rocks below.

The old man faces into the wind happily. He grins. "Always there is some wind blowing here. In the desert there is no wind. It is hot. But here on top it is nice and cool."

And there is water on the mountain top. The rock is pitted and hollowed out by the wind. In these natural pools there is water from the recent rains.

"No tourists come up here. Always this water is clean," the Tigua Governor says. He grins again.

"These are the Hueco Tanks," he says.

Hueco is the Spanish word for a hollow dish or earthen bowl. It just describes the basins of rock. The word "tank" is an old English word. It simply means a small pool of water. But the meaning of the Hueco Tanks is not as simple as the meaning of the two words. If it were, there would be no mystery.

In one of the caves down below there is a path that leads deep into the dark. Then it disappears.

The cave ends abruptly at a wall of rock that rises from its damp floor like a sheer and unsurmountable cliff. Hanging from the roof of the cave the spidery bats flutter in the darkness. There are hundreds of bats. Lizards slither about like shadows. It is a dungeon in the bowels of a mountain, a tomb where a stranger would be lost and might never find his way out.

Anyone who tried to hide inside the cave from an enemy would be trapped by the dead end amid the bats and lizards. He could not escape.

"No one knows it, but there is a way to get out of the cave. There is a secret way," the Tigua Governor says. "We know how."

He walks far into the cave. Where the wall of rocks blocks the way there is a thin glimmer of light in the darkness. It comes from high in the roof, beyond the perches of the bats. The roof of the cave inclines upward at a sharp angle, perhaps three hundred feet above the floor of the underground chamber. Where the old man has pointed, one can see sunlight.

There is a hole in the mountain!

If a man slithers like a lizard up the crevice between the wall and the roof, he would be able to climb through the hole in the mountain. The opening is like a window to the sky.

Years ago the ancestors of the Tiguas may have escaped from the Apaches through the hole. Their enemies were probably mystified by this disappearing act.

No one looking into the cave from the valley would know of the hidden passage. It is one of the Tiguas' secrets.

If it rains on the mountain top the water flows through the window to the sky and becomes an underground stream. On the roof of the cave the water drips, drop by drop, like blood dripping from a wound in the mountain. The creeping of the water and the fluttering of the bats would be enough to frighten most men out of the cave—if not out of their wits. To the Tigua Governor the cave is cool and comfortable, and almost cozy. He feels at home.

"You feel very nice here. You want to go to sleep right away," he says. "It's so cool."

Some of the caves in the mountains are so large that houses could be built inside of them. It is an underground world.

"There are many secret places," says the Tigua Governor. "There are big caves with open spaces where you can build things up and live. Very nice places to spend the whole day, maybe weeks. I can show you many places you will like to live in. You will like to stay there forever."

It was deep in one of these huge caves that the tribe came out of the Underworld, some say. God created the Tiguas there. That is a mysterious and holy place, some say.

Nonsense! say others. Everyone knows that the tribe came from the north on the long journey from the pueblo of Gran Quivira, in the mountains of New Mexico. The old Cacique always said, "And remember this: Our people came from Gran Quivira." There is no mystery about it, so why make a mystery of it?

The men who study these things, the experts on Indian life, think they know the truth. It is a myth that the tribe was created, they say. Scientifically it is impossible. Anyone who believes that must believe in magic.

One man who is a friend of the tribe and knows them well says that the Tiguas "have very little recollection of their origin and a common myth among them is that they originated in the Hueco Tanks." But it isn't so, he says.

"More likely, the myth originated from the fact that a group of Tiguas were taken to the Hueco Tanks some years ago to perform a ritual dance," he explains. "While there, they observed the Indian pictographs found in the Hueco Tanks and possibly misinterpreted these signs of Indian life as evidence of their origin." But it isn't so, he says.

So many people always think they know more about Indians than Indians know about themselves. The Indians are much too polite to laugh at them.

"We came from the Hueco Tanks. We came from Gran Quivira, too," the Tigua Governor insists. "We moved around. Lots of people do."

If it is a myth that the Tiguas believe in, it is a realistic myth. But then Indian myths are always realistic.

The lands in the Hueco Tanks are very much like the lands of the pueblo of Gran Quivira. Both are in circles of mountains in the midst of deserts. Both are in hidden valleys. Both are oases of once fertile fields and grass and water holes and secret caves. Both are like Gardens of Eden. Whether the Tiguas came from one place or the other place hardly matters. They are the same place.

And so the story that the Tiguas tell of their origins is not a fairy tale. It is an accurate memory of where they came from.

One thing is certain, when the stagecoaches rode into history, the white man gave the Hueco Tanks back to the deserts. He did not give it back to the Tiguas. Like a shroud of sand the desert blew over the hidden valley. It was forgotten for years.

No one wanted this wasteland except the Tiguas. And they were denied it.

Then the suburbs were invented. Land companies began to buy up the land of the Hueco Tanks all around the mountains. And the State of Texas thought how pleasant it would be if the Hueco Tanks were made into a State Park for the tourists.

"We used to have to pay one dollar to visit our own land," says the Tigua Governor. He sighs a bit ruefully. "We did not have one dollar.

"Now they say we do not have the land. The State of Texas and the real-estate companies have the land. Why? Because they take it away from us!" he says.

"I tell you what we have," the Governor of the Tiguas says. "We have nothing!"

VII

El Barrio de los Indios

The corn is tall in the suburbs. In the summer sun the ears of corn are heavy and the tassels shine like golden tinsel. Nowhere within the city limits of El Paso is there a cornfield quite like the one that grows behind the parking lot of the air-conditioned tribal office of the Tiguas.

Who owns the cornfield? "It belongs to the tribe. Everyone owns it," they say.

And that is how it is among the Tiguas. Everyone in the tribe shares whatever is left of their tribal life.

Living in a tribe is like living in a very large family. The family has to share its way of life or there is no family. In the tribe, when a man has good fortune he is expected to share his good fortune with those less fortunate. He disgraces the family if he doesn't. To the Tiguas, the successful man who keeps his success for himself is a failure.

"He is selfish" is their way of saying "He is not a real Tigua."

But that does not mean that everyone shares everything he owns. Sometimes a man must be alone.

It is a communal life, but just in some ways. They do not share their houses or their gardens. They do not share their belongings. A little family lives by itself within the larger family. Even in a tribe a man has to have privacy.

They do share their way of life and their beliefs. They share their joys and pains. They share their past and future.

And if someone in the tribe is sick, then everyone is expected to come and help. To bring food. To worry. To pray.

And if someone in the tribe is happy, then everyone comes to celebrate his happiness.

"Yesterday was my birthday. My brothers came to my house to dance for me," says Pablo Carbajal, the Lieutenant Governor of the Tiguas. He has tears in his eyes. "My brothers love me—my Indian brothers," he says.

His "brothers" may be his cousins. In the tribe the

families are often related to one another, but that is not what the Lieutenant Governor is talking about. When he talks of "my Indian brothers" he means all of the men of the tribe. He means everyone who is a Tigua is his brother.

In the Barrio de los Indios—the Town of the Indians, or Indiantown—where the Tiguas live, they do not have much left to share except their brotherhood and their memories and their poverty.

So poor is the Barrio de los Indios that the Tiguas say, "Even the rats are friendly."

The houses of the Tiguas are mostly huts of adobe mud. In these houses there are few of the simplest things that the poorest families in the ghettos have.

Many of the families have no electricity. They have no electric lights. No television sets. No radios. No refrigerators. No heating. Kerosene lamps have to be used for light. And wood-burning stoves are still used for cooking and warmth.

In most of the houses there is no running water. There is no fresh water to drink. There are no sinks, no bathtubs, no toilets. There is just the river, half a mile away.

A few years ago when the chairman of the Texas Commission on Indian Affairs visited the Tiguas he asked the Cacique, Jose Granillo, what his people needed the most.

"Water!" the Cacique said.

In the midst of the Barrio de los Indios there are huge canals, wide as the highways. These man-made rivers rush millions of gallons of water to irrigate the fields of Texas. None of this water is for the Tiguas. It is ironic. Hundreds of years before the Texas farmers came into the Rio Grande valley the Tigua farmers dug the first irrigation ditches in the area. Now they have no water.

The desert dust dries the eyes and the mouths. Everywhere the heat rises like dust.

Whenever it rains, however, there is too much water. The unpaved roads are full of mudholes and there are plenty of unpaved roads and there are no city sewers to drain the rain.

The mud is everywhere. Actually the roads are paved—with mud. The houses are built with mud. The walls are plastered with mud. The pots and dishes are made of mud. Even the ovens where the Tiguas bake their Indian bread are made of mud.

In the muddy yards of their mud houses the Tiguas have built outdoor ovens of mud, some of which are four feet high.

"If we could sell mud, we would be rich," says a Tigua teenager.

Lawyer for the tribe, Tom Diamond, says that the income of the average Tigua family is about $400 a year. That's less than $10 a week for an entire family.

Jose Granillo, the tribal chief, lives in a dark house of mud. He is a poor man. He too has no water, no electricity, and no heat. Inside his tiny hut the sparse furniture is mostly made of wooden crates and boxes, with a broken old bed on the earth floor. His house of mud is typical of the simple homes of many Tiguas.

In spite of their poverty the Tiguas do not protest. They do not march on city hall. They do not riot.

"We do not make troubles," says Miguel Pedraza, the Tigua Governor. "We do not beg for something by protests."

He is asked: What about the men of the tribe who fought in the guerrilla army of Pancho Villa during the Mexican Revolution? Luz Pedraza was one of the revolutionaries. Wasn't he your father?

"That was different," says Miguel Pedraza, with a gentle smile.

"My father did not march in protest to beg for something," he says. "It is not good to beg. It is not good to ask for anything. My father did not beg. He fought. That was different.

"We are proud. It is not dignified to beg and protest," says the Tigua Governor. "We are poor, so we help our brothers."

It is hard for the Tiguas to understand people who live only for themselves. That is "the way animals live," says the Tigua Governor. "Life is 'dog eat dog' some people say, but that sounds like 'people eat people' to me," he says.

"Are people dogs?" he asks.

"Everybody ought to be friendly, I think, with everybody. Everybody ought to treat everybody the same way he treats himself," says the Tigua Governor.

Brotherhood is not just a word to the tribe. It is the

way they live. Without the brotherhood of the large family of the tribe the little families of the Tiguas would not be able to survive the poverty of the Barrio de los Indios.

"We, the Tiguas, do not hate anybody at all. Some people hate us, but we don't hate. If your life is going to be happy, you have to love. No one can be happy with hate," says Pablo Carbajal, the Lieutenant Governor.

"Tell me, do your white brothers dance for you on your birthday?" he asks.

VIII

Medicine of the Sun

When a Tigua boy loses a tooth he throws it at the sun.

He throws it high into the sky, trying to come as close to the sun as he can. It seems foolish to the Tigua boy to hide his tooth under his pillow and wish upon it. What good will that do? The sun makes things grow. And the sun will grow his new tooth. So he offers his old tooth to the sun. But he throws it with a back-handed toss, for he has to be respectful of the sun and not hit it with his tooth.

"*Sol! Sol! Tome este diente y dame un otro mejor!*" he says in Spanish. "Sun! Sun! Take this tooth and give me a better one!"

In ancient times the old ones believed the sun was the father of life on earth. Of course they were right. Nothing would grow without the sun; it would be too cold. The earth would be a dark and dead hunk of dirt, lost in eternal night. Even the people would die.

Were not the children of the Aztecs then taught that the sun was God? In the schools of Mexico, long before Columbus was born, the school children recited this lesson:

> *The Sun is an eagle.*
> *He has arrows of fire.*
> *He is Lord of Time.*
> *He is a God.*
> *He makes things bright.*
> *He gives life.*

It has always been so. The sun in the desert gives life and gives death. Nothing is more holy in the pueblos of the Southwest than the sun.

So the Tiguas prayed to the Father Sun who sent his warmth to nourish the Mother Earth.

They believed they were the children of the Father Sun and the Mother Earth. They prayed to these Gods, who were parents of all life, by singing:

Mother in the Earth,
Father in the Sky,
We are your children;
We give you gifts of love.

And do the children of the Tiguas believe in the ways of their parents? Some do. Some don't. The boy who threw his tooth to the sun was praying in the old way. He was worshiping the sun, whether he knew it or not.

He would not have prayed to his dentist by singing:

Dentist! Dentist!
Take this tooth
And give me
A false tooth!

No one believes a dentist is a god. He may cure a toothache. But we know that a dentist, or a doctor, is not holy.

Some of the older people in the tribe have never been to a doctor in their lives. The Cacique, old Jose Granillo, remembers going to a doctor once, when he was a young man. He never went again. He is now a man of seventy.

The Cacique cures himself. In his hut, he keeps paper bags filled with herbs hanging on the wall. He gathers these herbs in the desert, as his ancestors did. Many of these ancient herbs contain chemicals that are used in modern medicines. So the old medicine man is not as old-fashioned as he seems.

"Nowadays our young people, they don't believe much in herbs. They don't believe in that," he says, and he shrugs. "But people like me, I still believe in herbs. Herbs can do you good, sometimes.

"Even if you drink a glass of water, it can do you good." He laughs.

He trusts in herbs, but he trusts in God more. The best medicine is neither the herbs of the medicine man nor the drugs of the doctor, he says; it is prayer.

"One thing I know for sure: God takes care of you all the time," says the Tigua Governor. "God takes care of you, or me, or everybody else. I myself, I depend on God."

The old man chuckles. "Am I healthy? Look at me! I haven't used the doctors too much. Back in 1959 I went to look at a doctor. Back in 1964 I went to look at another doctor. As far as I know, I didn't need them."

He has a youthful grin on his lips. In the edges of his eyes the skin is wrinkled with age, but his eyes are clear and his face is young and vigorous.

Some people need doctors, he says. He is not opposed to doctors—for others. "As far as I know there are two or three doctors who treat Tiguas in downtown El Paso," he says. "Some people go.

"Of course, I haven't seen one myself," he adds. "And I'm glad. I feel pretty good. I haven't needed the doctors, so far. Maybe later."

In the rainy spring of 1968 the old woman of the tribe, Margarita Carbajal, became very ill and had to be taken to a doctor. The aged woman was then ninety-eight. Now she lay in a coma, coughing. Her shrunken body heaved in the moist, hot desert air and her fever burned on her shriveled skin. She lay so still. She could barely breathe.

"She is dying," some said. But the Tigua Governor did not believe it.

Just a few days before, the old woman sat up in her bed and sang the tribal songs of her youth. Her memory was like a book.

"I will take her to the hospital in my car," the Tigua Governor said. There was no need to call the ambulance. "If there is a big emergency I can call the ambulance. But there is no emergency," he said. "So we'll use my car."

The old woman was only ninety-eight. He didn't see why everyone was so worried. After all, she had been sick before and had recovered.

"Besides, she is my aunt. So I'm going to take care of her myself," he said.

Love from one's family was as healthy a medicine as any the doctors in the hospital could give her, the Tigua Governor suggested. He would wrap her in love.

The old woman was lifted lovingly into the car by the men of the tribe. In the heavy heat of the summer afternoon, it was 120 degrees in the desert, they drove down the highway to the hospital. Some thought the old woman was dying. Some who waved good-by to her that day thought they would never see her again.

One year later Margarita Carbajal celebrated her ninety-ninth birthday.

She sang again. The matriarch of the tribe had survived the hospital. In front of her hut the people sang and prayed, to thank the gods. "Our herbs are strong," the Governor of the Tiguas said. "We make some strong medicines and drink them. We get by." And then he smiled, as if to say: "Love is the best medicine of all."

IX

The Talking Drum

In the yard the young boys are being taught to ''talk''
to the tribal drum. They practice their music lesson on
the empty gas tank of a junked car.

The Cacique is the music teacher. He sits on a
wooden crate as though it is a throne. In his red
beaded cap he wears the eagle feather of a chief. On
his lap he holds the empty gas tank, and he beats it
with his fist.

At the feet of the Cacique are empty beer cans. His

music students put pebbles into the beer cans and use them as rattles. The empty gas tank and beer can band of the Tiguas is one of the few in the country.

One by one the young boys take turns drumming on the empty gas tank.

The Cacique listens. He is a gentle but strict music teacher. If a boy drums a wrong note or dull tune, the old man does not yell at him. He says nothing. He merely makes a face like he has just swallowed a frog.

Laughing, the Cacique will show the awkward boy how it should be done. He beats the beat-up metal with quick but sharp thuds and thumps. The hollow metal booms like rolling thunder. Everyone jumps. "Fffud, fffud, fffud, VAROOM! Fffud, fffud, fffud, VAROOM!"

If a boy is to learn to beat the tribal drum, he has to learn the drumbeats by heart. There is no written music.

Fathers teach sons. The War Captain, Trinidad Granillo, has taught his son, Concepción, the old chants. When the time comes, the boy will teach his own son.

It is not easy to play religious music that has been played the same way for many hundreds of years. The songs are sung to God. His ears would be offended by an off-beat note. God is listening, say the Tiguas. There can be no mistakes. If the rhythm is wrong, their prayers may not be answered; for the beats of the drum are like the words of a mass.

The real tribal drum is sacred. If someone harms, or insults, or even misuses the drum, he may be struck dead by the anger of God.

One day a neighbor took the drum. He was not a Tigua, but a Mexican, they say. He wished to play a popular tune, that was all. Leaning on the wall of an adobe hut, in the shade, he was quietly beating the drum when a bolt of lightning crashed out of the sunny sky and hit the wall of the hut a few feet from where he was sitting. He was nearly killed, they say. He had offended God.

And that is why the young boys practice on an empty gas tank, not on the tribal drum, during an *ensaye*, or music lesson. It might be too dangerous if they played badly.

Someone who asks the name of the drum will be told it is the *tombe*, which means "drum" in Spanish, or the *wa-chee-ro*, which means "drum" in Tiwa. But that is not what the drum is called.

The drum has a personal name. It is a he. He is known as Juan, or John.

Juan has his own personality. He has a soul. The old drum is even known to get hungry, they say. When that happens, a little corn meal that has been blessed is fed to the drum through a small hole in its side. Then Juan is happy.

Every now and then, one of the men of the tribe breathes the breath of life into the drum by touching his mouth to the small hole in its side and blowing into its insides. They say it is the War Captain who does this, though no one sees him do it. He breathes his own life into the drum, they say.

The breath of many men has filled the drum in this way. For the tribal drum of the Tiguas is centuries old.

Long ago a log was cut from a tree on the Mountains of the Apple. It was hollowed out and decorated. The skin of a deer was stretched over the open ends and tied with thongs. And so the sacred drum of the Tiguas was created.

No one remembers when the drum was made. There is no memory that old.

When the Old People came down from the Mountains of the Apple, they brought their drum with them. That was in 1675. Wherever they have gone, it has gone with them on their migrations. That is what some say.

On the faded drumhead the history of the tribe has been "written" by the hands of many generations of wise men. The beat of the drum has spoken of all the things that have ever happened to the Tiguas. It has greeted thousands of dawns and deaths, announced births of infants and fiestas, summoned the warriors to battle and celebrated their heroic deeds and defeats.

The drummers are now dead and forgotten. But the drum has not forgotten. It is a history book of sounds.

History is not told in words alone. It may be told by a dance, or by the lines on the face of the land, or in the rings of an old tree, or by drawings in a cave. The story of the past is told in many ways to those who know how to listen and see and "read" these unwritten signs.

And the drum is like a wise old man. And he remembers everything. That is why they "talk to the drum." That is why they listen when the drum "talks" to them.

When the Cacique or the War Captain or the Governor of the tribe has to go to a meeting, he first has a "talk" with his drum. He asks the drum what to do. The drum tells him, they say, "which way to go and what to say."

Old Alton Griffin, who is the Superintendent of the Tiguas for the State of Texas, says: "They will never appear at any business meeting of government of any type, or at a Congressional hearing to give testimony, without first having a ceremony where they 'talk' to the drum. Unless they do this they will not consider the meeting as being official or binding, or of any importance whatsoever.

"When asked about their conversations with the drum, they simply reply, 'That is between us and the drum,'" says Griffin.

One day, in 1968, the tribal leaders were asked to travel to the capital of Texas to talk with the leaders of the state legislature. The lawmakers were considering a proposal to officially recognize the tribe. So the Cacique, the War Captain and the Governor went to Austin. They took a room in a downtown motel.

At dawn the guests in the motel were woken by the beating of a drum. The sleeping tourists may have thought they had been dreaming about the old West. Were the Indians on the warpath in the motel? Or in their nightmares?

It was merely the Tiguas. They were having a "talk" with their drum. They thought it might be wise to listen to the wisdom of the past before talking to the state legislature of Texas. Who knows, it might help.

The legislators may have eavesdropped on their conversation. For the State of Texas, soon after talking to the Tiguas, voted for the first time in history to officially recognize the tribe and to appropriate money to help them.

In celebration, the Cacique painted the nose of Governor John Connally of Texas with ocher war paint.

Until that time no government had recognized the tribe's existence. The officials had always ignored it. Now the Democrats and Republicans in Congress both decided to help the Tiguas.

On April Fools' Day, in 1968, Senator Ralph Yarborough of Texas introduced into the United States Senate a bill, S. 1958, that would give the Tiguas official recognition. He spoke with irony:

"Considering how many other tribes, groups and bands of Indians in the country have been recognized by the United States, it is virtually impossible to explain how the Tiwas have been missed up to this time," said the Senator.

"They are dying out," he warned. Unless the

Congress acts, he said, "one day the beat of the tom-tom bidding the Tiguas to assemble will be only an echo."

His proclamation proclaimed:

"Whereas Indians now living in El Paso County, Texas, are descendants of the Tiwa Indians of the Ysleta (Isleta) del Sur Pueblo, a branch separated in 1682 from the Tiwa-speaking Isleta Pueblo of central New Mexico; and

"Whereas the Ysleta del Sur Pueblo founded the first permanent Tiwa settlement in Texas, at Isleta, in 1682, where the tribe still lives today; and

"Whereas the Tiwa Indians of Ysleta del Sur today, known as the Tigua Indians, have a distinctive speech, appearance and culture, and a well-organized tribal civil organization, all of which can be traced to the original Tiwa Indians of the Ysleta del Sur Pueblo; and

"Whereas these people are naturally and understandably proud of their heritage and desirous of establishing their social status and preserving their racial history; Now, therefore

"*Be it enacted by the Senate and House of Representatives of the United States of America in Congress assembled,* That the Indians now living in El Paso County, Texas . . . shall from and after the ratification of this Act, be known and designated as Tiwa Indians of Ysleta, Texas. . . ."

Congress passed the act. The President of the

United States, Lyndon Baines Johnson, signed it into law. The Tiguas officially existed.

If someone honors the Tiguas they will honor him in return. And so the tribe packed their old tribal drum into the tribal stationwagon, piled their luggage and costumes on the roof and set off for Washington, D.C., with their finest young dancers, to dance in honor of the Congress of the United States and the President.

They danced on the Capitol Mall. They baked Indian bread on the grass near the Smithsonian Institution in honor of the occasion.

Lieutenant Governor of the tribe, Pablo Carbajal, went along with the young dancers. He was happy about the honor that the Tiguas had been given, but not very.

He was asked if he thought now that the tribe had been recognized the government would help them.

"Nobody ever helped us," he said. "They say now the government will help us. If they do, it is good. If they don't, it doesn't matter. . . . We have been here so long, so long. We will just go on," said Pablo Carbajal.

The Governor of the Tiguas, who stood nearby, nodded in agreement.

But weren't they happily surprised that the tribe had been recognized after so many years?

"No, we knew it would happen," the Tigua Governor said.

How could they know? How could they be so confident, when no one had done anything for the Tiguas before?

"We knew." The Tigua governor smiled. "We have the drum."

Top: The Tiguas' cemetery dates back to 1680, and there is no room left in it to bury the dead. *Center:* This small cornfield is shared by everyone in the tribe. The corn is used for religious purposes and, of course, to eat. *Below:* In the home of Jose Granillo, Cacique, there is no electricity, no running water, no toilet facilities and no television. *Photo: Tigua Tribe (Lee Cain)*

Top left: The huge canal that runs through the suburbs of El Paso where the Tiguas live; a typical adobe Tigua home is on the right. *Photo: Tigua Tribe (Lee Cain). Left below:* ''We are Tiguas!'' these boys said as they posed by the canal. *Below:* These young boys of the Tigua tribe are learning how to drum by hand, on an empty auto gas tank. *Photo: Tigua Tribe (Lee Cain)*

Left: Miguel Pedraza, Tribal Governor, and the tribal drum. *Below:* Tribal leaders standing by tribal stationwagon during farewells to those going to Washington. On the right is Pablo Carbajal, Lieutenant Governor, and next to him, Miguel Pedraza.

X

The Scalping Song

"Ho-o-wi-na! A-ye-a-a! Ho-o-wi-na! A-ye-a-a!"

The Scalping Song was sung softly. The singers were friendly.

In the banquet hall of the sedate Hotel Cortez, on the plaza of downtown El Paso, the tribal war chants are not heard—very often. The men of the tribe sang almost silently into the microphone. It was the old song that was sung loudly when the warriors had fought and defeated their enemy. But that was long ago. And it was an unusual song to sing in the banquet hall of a busy hotel.

It was in victory that they sang. After hundreds of years of living nearly invisibly in the suburbs of the city, the Lost Tribe of Tiguas had been "discovered."

They had been invited to a meeting in the Hotel Cortez of the "United Nations" of the tribes, the National Congress of American Indians. Leaders of four hundred thousand Indians in one hundred tribes were honoring the United States government's recognition of the little tribe of Tiguas. Once again the Lost Tribe would be united with their brothers.

So the grandsons of the warriors sang their Scalping Song. They sang it as their ancestors had in the old days when they had triumphed in battle against the Apaches.

"*Ho-o-wi-na! A-ye-a-a! Ho-o-wi-na! A-ye-a-a!*" On the microphones of the banquet hall the Scalping Song sounded especially eerie. Everyone listened in silence.

The song has been secret. No one but the Tiguas know the words.

In one of the pueblos far to the north, where tourists are invited, the people sing a Scalping Song that is like that of the Tiguas. The words of that song are something like this:

> *Enemy youth!*
> *It is your fault alone*
> *That now you die*
> *Fallen by your house*
> *With mud-streaked thighs;*

Now your mouths
Are stopped!
Ho-o-wi-na! A-ye-a-a!
The next scalp!

Why did they sing this?

Perhaps it was because the President of the National Congress of American Indians was an Apache. He was Wendell Chino, the tribal leader of the Mescalero Apache tribe. Years ago these Apaches had been the enemies of the Tiguas.

In the old days the Apaches had raided and helped destroy the great pueblo of the Tiguas, the city of Gran Quivira. Hundreds of people had been killed. The Tiguas had never forgotten.

Now the tribal leader of these Apaches was honoring them. Was that why they sang their Scalping Song —in victory?

Someone asked the Tiguas, What is this song you sang?

They smiled. They did not know, they said. It was a song that was so old that no one knew what it was, they said.

"I know it," said Andrew Abeita, the Governor of the Isleta Pueblo of New Mexico, who was attending the meeting in the Hotel Cortez. He recognized it as an old Scalping Song, he said.

Someone asked the Tiguas, Is that so?

They shrugged. They did not really know, they said. And they smiled, a bit secretively.

XI

The Warrior Chiefs
of the
Peaceful People

The little bird flew into the path of the car on the superhighway. And there was a quiet thud when the few ounces of feathers hit the two tons of steel. Into the sky the bird's feathers flew like an exploding firecracker. Roaring down the superhighway at seventy miles an hour, the driver did not stop. The little bird was dead.

"Wait! Wait!" one of the tribal elders in the car cried. "Let us stop!"

In the back seat of the speeding car were the Cacique, the War Captain and the Governor of the Tiguas. The Governor had cried out with anguish for the bird. He was very upset.

"We must help that little bird," he said. "We hit it."

"He's dead," the driver said dourly.

Lawyer for the tribe, Tom Diamond, was driving, and he was in a hurry to get home. It had been a long ride, nearly five thousand miles. The leaders of the tribe were coming home from the ceremonies in Washington, D.C. The old men had refused to fly in an airplane. So the lawyer had driven them all the way, and he was driving them all the way home again. He wasn't going to stop for a dead bird.

That evening they came to a plush motel in Austin, Texas, the state capital, where they would stay the night.

As soon as the car stopped at the motel, the three tribal elders jumped out. They ran around to the front bumper where the little bird had been hit. It was the Governor who reached his hand under the chrome grille. He took out the mangled body of the bird. And held it gently in his opened palm. The three tribal elders, the Cacique, the War Captain and the Governor, stood there in a circle, sadly smoothing the bird's crushed feathers. They were talking softly.

One of the uniformed motel attendants came up to them. "Hey! What you got there?" he asked.

He was shown the little treasure.

"It's nothing but a dead bird," the man in uniform shrugged. "You better throw that thing in the trash." He walked away, shaking his head in disgust.

"You hear that! He said throw it in the trash!" the Governor exclaimed in disbelief.

"Sure," the lawyer said. "What else you going to do with a dead bird? You going to hold a funeral service?"

Lovingly the Tigua Governor cupped his fingers about the lump of feathers. He mournfully carried the dead bird through the lobby of the motel to the room the lawyer had reserved for them. The three tribal leaders sat and whispered among themselves for several moments. It was a private conference; they ignored the lawyer.

"Well?" the lawyer said finally. "Have you decided what you are going to do with that thing?"

Quietly the tribal leaders walked to the door. The Tigua Governor was still holding the dead bird in his palm. He softly said, "We will bury it."

And somewhere in a garden of plastic flowers and fake grass of a plush motel in the capital of Texas there is a grave of a little bird that was killed on the superhighway.

Life is holy to the Tiguas. Not just man's life, but all of life on earth is holy to them. They believe that everything is sacred. It is their religion. The way some people believe that God is in their church, the Tiguas believe that God is everywhere. He is in a little bird.

He is in the tiniest and ugliest of God's creatures. He is in every living thing on earth. And every thing on earth is living.

Is a stone living?

"Yes, if God is in a stone," says Miguel Pedraza, the Tigua Governor. "If a man worships a stone because he sees God there, who am I to say no?

"I believe the sun is God. The wind is God. The water is God. The earth is God," says the Tigua Governor. "Everything around us is the same God.

"So I think God is everyplace," he says. "Even in a spider."

He does not say the insects are gods, but he says the spirit of God is in the insects. So he respects even a spider.

"If I see a spider coming in the door of my house, I pick him up and put him outside. He is free," he says. "But I don't kill him.

"Little insects, or little animals, whatever you call them, have the same right to live as I do," he says. "So that's why I don't kill anything any more. I just can't do it. The way I feel is, we all have a right to live. Don't you think?"

Some of the Tiguas believe in life so strongly that they will not kill a living thing. If all of life is holy, then killing must be unholy, they say.

Jose Granillo, the Cacique, feels this way. He will not kill a bug, they say.

They tell the tale of how one day the Cacique knelt beside the superhighway. In his old, shriveled hand he held a piece of paper shaped like a scoop. He was looking for something.

"What are you doing?" he was asked.

He was scooping up worms that had crawled onto the highway, in the path of the cars. He knelt inches from the rushing traffic that zoomed by his bent body. The Cacique lifted the worms from the cement and let them wiggle away into the safety of the grass.

"Even the worms have a life to live," he explained.

The reverence of life that the Tiguas feel sometimes makes them do things that may seem strange. In our hectic way of life we often ignore, or do not care about, life other than our own. Life is cheap, we say. Who worries about worms when men kill one another so easily?

In the old days the Tiguas were not so peaceful. They fought for survival. And they fought hard, so hard that they were usually on the winning side; they survived.

They fought against the conquistadors, and then they fought alongside the knights of Spain, with soldiers from the other pueblos. They fought the Apaches, and they defeated a band led by the famous warrior, Victorio, at *Paso Viejo* (the Old Pass). They fought the Comanches at *Sierra Hueco* (Hollow in the Sawtoothed Mountain). They fought as Indian scouts for the U.S. Army's Tenth Cavalry, a troop of Negro frontier soldiers. They fought in the army of General Francisco "Pancho" Villa during the Mexican

Revolution. They fought for the United States in almost every major war.

Miguel Pedraza says his grandfather was an Indian scout who fought the Apaches. His father rode with Pancho Villa. "Quite a few people from here went and helped Pancho Villa," says the Tigua Governor. "I have an old photograph of my father when he was fighting in the Mexican Revolution."

And his son is a veteran of the paratroopers. He is a modern warrior.

In spite of the fighters in the history of his family the Governor of the Tiguas no longer believes in wars.

"Wars? I think the wars are no good at all," he says. "It's just too much misunderstanding. One thing I know, the soldiers on each side, they shoot each other, but they don't know what for. I'm not too sure about everything, but I don't feel they are doing the right thing. No, they are wrong."

He says, "I don't like wars."

When the Tiguas fought it was because they were attacked, he says. "They fought for something. They had a reason. But I have no reason to fight," he says.

Once the Tigua Governor was a hunter. He hunted every animal in the desert. He doesn't even like to hunt now.

"We shot rabbits, yes. But I don't like to shoot rabbits no more," he says.

"I shot rabbits, shot deer, shot animals. I quit. I don't know how, but I quit. I don't like to kill animals any more. I don't like to kill even a mouse. Like I say, if there is a mouse around my place I just catch him and let him go. That's the kind of Indian I am," he says.

The son of the Governor feels the way his father does. He was a paratrooper for eight years. He is a hardened veteran who was decorated for his service to his country. And he is proud of his military career. But he will not kill.

"He don't want to use any more guns," Miguel Pedraza says of his son.

"You could get a job with the police, I told him. 'No, daddy,' he said, 'I don't want to have anything to do with guns no more.' He quit it, too," the father says. "Maybe he have the same notion as me. We don't like to shoot live things no more.

"We don't like to kill," he says.

XII

The Land of the Tiguas

"I love to drive," says the young Tigua.

Like a hunter riding through a herd of wild buffalo, he drives his old car down the highway into the wildest traffic with bravery and caution. He is an expert driver. He knows his jalopy the way a cowboy knows his horse, for his life depends on his skill in handling his metal steed amid the stampede of trucks and cars.

He is doing just one thing wrong. The young Tigua is driving without a driver's license.

It is against the law to drive without a license in the

city. He knows this. Every so often he will be fined. He knows this too. He will pay his fine obediently and drive away, until the next time, when he will be fined once more, and have to pay.

Some of the men of the tribe do this many times. Why are they so stubborn?

A neighbor says: "It's a matter of the Indians' pride. They would rather be fined for driving without a license and pay the fine than get a driver's license from strangers."

"Yes, that's how I feel," says the young Tigua. "I don't want to break any laws. But why do I have to get a license to drive on our own land?

"We don't ask the Texans to get licenses to drive on our land," he says. "So why do we have to get licenses to drive on their land? Especially since *their* land is really *our* land, anyway."

Once, it is true, the tribe of Tiguas did own the city of El Paso. That was hundreds of years ago, but they have not forgotten.

In the grassy fields along the river they built what was to become the first city in Texas. They named it *Ysleta del Sur*, Isleta of the South, after the pueblo they left in 1680. At that time there were just a few huts of reeds and mud in the valley where the Mansos Indians had little farms. The sons of the builders of the great city of Gran Quivira were not satisfied with such houses, for they were skilled architects and construction workers. And they built a new city.

They built the first Christian church in Texas. Long

before the mission church that became famous as the Alamo was thought of, the Tiguas' mission was a sturdy reality.

It so impressed the Royal Governor, Don Diego de Vargas, that in the name of the King of Spain, Charles II, he dedicated the church in 1691 as the *Mission de Corpus Christi de los Tihuas de Ysleta.*

On a stone marker in front of the old church site the Texas State Highway Commission has honored this "First Mission and Pueblo (City) in Texas." In the church itself the priest hands out a "Short History of Ysleta Mission" that describes how the "First Log Church (later Ysleta)" was built by the Tiguas in 1680.

In 1751 the King of Spain recognized the faith and good works of the Tiguas by granting them possession of the entire city of El Paso.

The Ysleta Grant, it is believed, was for nearly thirty-six square miles. Some businessmen have estimated that the land would be worth $400,000,000 to the Tiguas if they still owned it. The poor Tiguas would all be millionaires.

Once the Tiguas were farmers. In the river valley their farms covered all of the city. They plowed and seeded the desert. And for hundreds of years they made the desert bloom. They have good memories of those years.

"I remember when I was a boy we worked in my grandfather's fields," says the Governor. "He had big fields. We worked together then. We helped one another. It was good then."

Now, they are farmers without farms. They have lost almost all their lands to the strangers. They were stolen from them. All they have left are their little houses and gardens. Soon they may lose these lands too, for they have no money to pay the real estate taxes the city demands from time to time.

"All we have left is a little bit of mud holes," says the Governor.

Not too long ago the United States recognized that the Tiguas owned all the land in the city. Legally the tribe might still own El Paso.

When the Treaty of Guadalupe-Hidalgo was signed, in 1848, by the governments of the United States and Mexico, the rights to all the lands owned by the former Mexican citizens living in the newly conquered territory were guaranteed by our government. The Ysleta Grant of the Tiguas was protected by that pledge.

The State of Texas promised to protect the Tiguas, too. By the Land Act of 1854 the legislature of Texas officially recognized the "Spanish Grant of 1751," the Ysleta Grant. It was the Tiguas' land, they said. No one could take it away. And the State Land Commissioner was ordered to give a patent for the land to the tribe.

But he forgot. Somehow the Commissioner forgot about the order for twenty years.

In Texas, after the railroad came to the West, there was a land boom. The dry desert became valuable. Land prices zoomed upwards, like clouds of dust. And the towns suddenly were full of land speculators, carpetbaggers, and real-estate dealers, some honest and some crooked.

The sleepy town of El Paso became a booming railroad center. It was then that someone remembered that the Tiguas owned the city.

Something had to be done! The Texas legislature changed its mind. It no longer was interested in protecting the lands of the Tiguas. Cleverly, with a just slightly illegal sleight of hand, it passed the "Special Act of 1871" that by-passed the "Act of 1854" and abolished the town of Ysleta. The old town no longer existed and a new town was voted into existence.

No one told the citizens. No election was held in the town. No one bothered to ask the Tiguas. The land speculators and new settlers were declared citizens of the new town. And they quickly patented the land in their names.

Land was bought and sold by these strangers who had never lived on it. Nor farmed it. In no time the Tiguas' lands were almost all stolen and sold. The tribe, most of whom could not even read English, hardly knew what was happening.

After all, how could someone they had never even met sell their land? It made no sense to them.

In 1874, when the land was all gone, the Texas legislature voted the new town of Ysleta out of existence. The now-you-see-it, now-you-don't town disappeared as it had appeared, without any vote by the citizens of Ysleta, the Tiguas.

"Well, it may have been just a little unconstitutional," says a lawyer in El Paso, with a rueful smile.

More recently the city of El Paso decided to extend its city limits to include Ysleta. The mud houses of the Tiguas, all they have left, were to be subject to real-estate taxes. Since the Tiguas have little land and little income, they hardly can afford to pay these taxes.

One by one the houses of the founding fathers of the city were to be taken away for back taxes by the newest city fathers. It was the ultimate irony.

The lawyer for the tribe argued that the city should not tax the land of the Tiguas. It was granted "by the King of Spain to the inhabitants of Ysleta in the year 1751," he says. And: "All historical references indicate that the inhabitants of Ysleta were the Tigua Indian tribe." He cites the recognition by the United States, and the State of Texas, of these land rights. He recites the sordid story of the "unconstitutional act" by which "substantially all the land [was given] to non-Indians."

Curiously, on hearing this history the tax collectors lost interest in their back taxes.

If the Tiguas were forced to go to court to defend their homes, they might try to reclaim their lost and stolen lands. Who knows who would then end up owning the city of El Paso?

"You know what I think?" says the young Tigua who drives without a driver's license. "Someday maybe the Texans will have to get their driver's licenses from us!"

XIII

The Hunt for the Extinct Deer

At the house of the War Captain the men gather again.
Not to dance, but to hunt.

Rifles in hand, they wait patiently. It is early in the
morning. The hunters are sleepy and stand about
yawning. But the excitement of the hunt is in their
eyes. The Cacique has begun the ceremony to bless
the hunters. He prays, and the men listen to him. The
men have old rifles. One man has a Winchester, the
kind of gun that was popular on the frontier in the
1870s. His gun needs a thorough blessing.

In the hands of the hunters are Enfield rifles from World War I, buckshot guns and modern Army surplus rifles.

"They have the damnedest collection of shootin' irons you ever saw," says Alton Griffin, the State of Texas Superintendent for the Tiguas, who is going along on the hunt. "Anything that can shoot. They even have some real hunting rifles."

Soon there are fifty men and boys waiting for the hunt to begin. They are ready to go into the desert.

In the old days the War Captain was in charge of the hunting. He still is. He has to round up the cars and trucks and make sure the tribal station wagon is ready. The guns are not his responsibility, for every man has his own, but he has to see to it that the hunters do not shoot each other, as hunters too often do. Most important of all, he has to be sure the prayers are said and the hunt is properly blessed.

When the War Captain is ready he gives the signal. The hunters head into the desert.

It is a strange hunting party. The caravan of cars stretches down the highway. Instead of ponies decorated with war paint, the Tiguas ride in modern cars with automatic shifts. The Day-Glo bumper stickers are the fiercest thing about these hunters, especially the ones that say PUT A TIGER IN YOUR TANK and REGISTER TO VOTE.

Along the road there are jackrabbits. They hop

wildly as the cloud of dust from the cars stirs them from their hiding places in the sagebrush.

"Chili-ha-ha! Hop! Hop!" yells the War Captain when he sees the jackrabbits. Everybody laughs.

The hunters are not very warlike. It is not like the old days when the hunt was a matter of life and death.

Years ago when the hunters went to the *Huecos* it was not so easy. The men hunted then for all their meat, and if the hunters got none, the tribe had none to eat. So the hunt was warlike; it had to be.

There was no road in the desert then. Just a wagon path.

"I remember when we went in wagons and on horses," says Miguel Pedraza, the Tigua Governor. "Some of the men rode the horses. The families went in the wagons. Everybody went, the whole family. Those days it took a long time to cross the desert. I remember one time we went there with my grandpa and grandma. We stayed there about fifteen days to go hunting.

"I remember they killed deer, killed antelope. We come home loaded with jerky meat. You know, what we call dried meat," he says.

"Nowadays it is not that way." Pedraza sighs. "We can go there in thirty minutes. We stay just a little while in the shade, feel the cool air, hunt a little, then drive home. So it's just like a picnic. There's no more good hunting around. There's no more deer."

If there are no more deer why do they go hunting?

Where do they hunt for these extinct deer?

The Tigua Governor winks. "A little way off we have a big place to hunt deer. No one knows about it. It is not in the *Huecos*. It is a little secret."

Where is this "big place"? He will not say. He doesn't go there himself because "I don't hunt," he says.

In the deserts to the north of the *Huecos* there is a "little secret, big place"—the Missile Range of the White Sand Proving Ground and the Fort Bliss Target Ranges. The hunters, if they go near there, have to be careful lest they become accidental targets of these more modern hunters.

One young Tigua says with bravado, "We were here first. So we are not afraid to go into the desert. It was our hunting ground before the soldiers came."

That bravery will not protect him from the missiles, however.

In camp on the first afternoon of the hunt some of the men come to Superintendent Griffin and say, We can't camp way out here without meat to eat. We have to go get some meat!

"Why sure," says Griffin. "Go shoot something!"

A few of the men go off on foot. They walk into the desert. In a little while they come back with a doe they have shot. They skin it with penknives. And they roast it right there, over a fire of mesquite tree branches and old wood they have found lying around.

The fire is crackling, the venison is crisp and tasty and everyone sleeps well that night.

In the morning a hunting party decides to go farther out into the desert. They go on a long hunt beyond the mountains, where the unknown and dangerous desert beckons. Many men have disappeared in those vast seas of uncharted sand.

Beyond the sunrise, in the midst of nowhere, they shoot a buck. It is nine miles back to camp. At first they think they will have to abandon their game. Then they have an idea.

One of the hunters finds the branch of a cottonwood tree. He ties the hoofs of the buck to the dead branch. Like the hunters would have done centuries ago, they lift the branch to their shoulders, the buck hanging head downward, and they begin the long walk back to camp.

They walk for nine miles through the desert. It takes all day.

"Nine miles! Nine miles in the desert! That's a long walk! It is like living back in the 1800s," says State Superintendent Griffin. "These people are something."

In the suburbs of the city where they live the Tiguas may be a Lost Tribe. But in the desert where there are no street signs, no roads, no policemen to point the way, they are not at all lost.

They know every rock, every cave, every water hole, every mountain. They know the names of every plant, every herb, every wild beast, every species of snake. And they know their names in three languages —Spanish, English and Tiwa. Not merely do they know everything in the desert, but they have their own familiar names for them. Like the nicknames of friends.

An arroyo, or gully, that seems desolate and frightening to a stranger is as familiar as an old friend to them. The history of the desert is their own history.

Says an old Tigua: "It is like going to visit relatives to come to these mountains. Here is my family."

Hundreds of years ago the gods created the Tiguas in the *Huecos*, they say. It is told and retold by the old men how this was done; for the legends of the tribe's founding fathers are told and retold like the legends of the heroes of the American Revolution are retold every year in school.

The hunting grounds of the tribe were given to them by the gods, they say. One does not give up such a gift easily.

No one can convince the Tiguas that the land is no longer theirs by showing them a real-estate deed. It is just a piece of paper to them.

"Did they get the deed from God?" asks the Tigua Governor.

When the men go hunting they do so to honor the memory of their forefathers. It is not just to get meat. That is why they hunt in the old ways.

Even now, they do not hunt jackrabbits with guns. If they go on a rabbit hunt they use long sticks with sharpened points. The weapons are like the ancient spears that hunters used before men knew how to make spearheads of stone or flint. Yet the Tiguas, who own rifles and who know about efficient modern weapons, still hunt rabbits with these wooden sticks.

Running through the sagebrush, yelling and whistling, they chase the rabbits into their holes. Once the rabbits have been trapped, the hunters poke their sticks into the burrows and spear them.

Hunting in these old ways is like living in the old days. One way of remembering one's memories is by reliving them.

Long ago in the grassy hollows of the *Hueco* Mountains the families farmed fields of corn and squash. Women sang as they ground cornmeal in stone troughs. Children played by the hidden pools. Men hunted for deer and antelope and fought off intruders. The old people cooled themselves in the winds of the caves on the hottest days.

And the horses ran wild in the hidden pastures. There were no fences.

When the tribe lived there they lived in peace. That's what they now believe. It was idyllic. So it now seems. The oasis of the Tiguas was an island in the burning desert, a sanctuary where their memories are as beautiful as fables.

It is not a memory that the Tiguas, living in the slums of the suburbs, will forget.

"My people used to live there! We know that!" says Miguel Pedraza, the Governor of the Tiguas. "Not to go there, but to live there. It's ours, this earth. Nowadays everybody claims, 'This land belongs to me! This land belongs to me!' "

He scoffs at those who say they own the earth. "God owns this earth," he says.

"We people have been here for so long. We do not mean we own this earth. But one thing we know for sure: we have been here first. So now we are in trouble to get these *Huecos* back. We are going to get them back," the Tigua Governor says. He has a determined but quiet look in his eyes.

"Little by little, we are going to get our earth back," he says. "I hope."

The abandoned hacienda that may someday be the Tigua Tribal Cultural Center, if the tribe can buy it, as they wish to. Now the Tiguas use two small rooms as tribal headquarters. Built in the 1700s, the hacienda was used by Pershing's cavalry when it invaded Mexico in 1917. The Tiguas, then, fought on the side of the Mexicans. *Photo: Tigua Tribe (Lee Cain)*

Index